Bound Stone

poems by

Colleen Anderson

Finishing Line Press
Georgetown, Kentucky

Bound Stone

ACKNOWLEDGMENTS

Grateful acknowledgment is given to the publications where the following poems
have appeared:

Kestrel, Spring 1993, and *Wild Sweet Notes: 50 Years of West Virginia Poetry*, 2000:
    "Bob Thompson at the Piano"
Carolina Quarterly, Winter 1986 : "Calhoun County, September"
Wild Sweet Notes: 50 Years of West Virginia Poetry, 2000: "Huckleberries"
Passager, Spring 2001: "On Getting a Late Start," "Waterfall in Winter"
Kestrel: "The Back Way," "Undressing One Another"
WPFW 89.3 Poetry Anthology, 1992: "Transplanting Ferns"
Arts & Letters, Spring 2000: "We Talk at Night," "Watermark"

Publisher: Leah Maines

Editor: Christen Kincaid

Cover Art: Bound stone by Del Webber

      Photograph by Colleen Anderson

Author Photo: Colleen Anderson

Cover Design: Colleen Anderson

Printed in the USA on acid-free paper.
Order online: www.finishinglinepress.com
    also available on amazon.com

Author inquiries and mail orders:
Finishing Line Press
P. O. Box 1626
Georgetown, Kentucky 40324
U. S. A.

Table of Contents

We Talk at Night

And why do we confess
except to conjure what
we used to be? It's not
real, but perhaps will pass

for real. What else to do,
when everything that's gone
before is gone? Go on,
go on, make something new,

the heart insists. It's what
we do. It's what we are
about, while we are here.
And call it love, or art.

Waterfall in Winter

because we'd walked
    all that way to visit
        the waterfall kindly
            came home with us
                whole and trembling
                    inside our bodies

oh transparent lip
    of anticipation and
        awful ache of gravity
            oh radiant plunge
                to foam and tumble
                    the river's long laughter

some afterfalls some
    quaking smaller pools
        then sweet sad singing
            shallow over pebbles
                plush silence of moss
                    deep grove of dreaming

out in the darkness
    in the welling fog
        the deer lay down
            the trees forgot us
                the careless waterfall
                    never stopped laughing

Overcast with Freezing Rain

I can't recall a winter like this one.
Before one blizzard softens into thaw,
another seizes us and pins us down.
We are encased in ice, suspended in *now*,
you by your woodstove, melting snow in a pot,
pipes ruptured, your life a shambles, you say,
I in my attic, cupping my ear for what
remains unfrozen: sound. A laugh. A sigh.
We talk about love, not in relation to
anything real, not in relation to us;
perhaps so as not to forget the word,
the liquid syllable, like melted snow,
infused with a promise of what there is
to hope for. The garden. That red-breasted bird.

After a Weekend in the Country

I tell you more than once, you drive too fast,
and you do. Curving downhill, your tires shear
the February slush. Even your fear
is young, not yet defined by what you've lost.
Slow, for my sake.

And yet, it isn't fear. I want to make
it last, this afternoon, this winter ride
through cottonwood and sycamore, beside
the Williams River. I want to take
all I can hold

from all I see: the subtle colors of cold
weather, the lichen and the moss, the way
bare branches form a brittle froth of grey
that deepens into mauve in the mountain's fold;
a fringe of sedge

clinging, seemingly rootless, to a ledge;
three fishermen in flannel shirts, who stare
into the water's churn and flash; and there,
block-lettered on a sign at river's edge,
CATCH AND RELEASE.

Well, I suppose it all comes down to this,
I say. And you, my scientist, confirm
that even our small, wise cells perform
exactly so. A breath's a masterpiece
of take and give.

It's one way to define the verb "to live,"
perhaps: to trade what is for what's to come.
My body knows that living's not a sum
of numbered intervals. The heart's a sieve
and not a bowl.

My body understands. Is it my soul
that keeps a stubborn ledger sheet of loss,
and mourns the fallen tree beneath the moss,
and never quite achieves that graceful goal,
catch and release?

On Getting a Late Start

How light drains from the day: amber to blue
to umber, even the creek's glimmer gone
to a bronze throb, a muscle pulsing through
a skin of snow, on skeleton of stone.
We cross it three times or more as we go
up the mountain, leaving behind our own
running stitch of tracks, as if to sew
the banks together. As we walk, the moon
swims up and up and up through shreds of cloud
and latticework of trees. We reach the crest
in silence. Not that we have nothing to say—
rather, I think, no need to say aloud
how good this is, what we would have missed
had we started earlier in the day.

Undressing One Another

We unlace language, too,
discard work-worn words
to touch what's under:
living, sinuous sound,
naked and profound,
bliss and fear and wonder
woven in complex chords
we didn't know we knew.

Bound Stone

For Michael Davis

The beauty isn't in the choice of stone
(a freckled, putty-grey, slightly off-round
found object, a palm-sized half-pound
of not-even-semi-precious rock) but in
the steady, deep attention to this one
among the many—not unlike the bond
between ourselves, my necessary friend,
the way we wrap ourselves with what we've known
together, year on year. And the koan:
A smooth, grey stone with bamboo twined around
it in a basket weave is no more bound
than a soul is closed inside a cage of bone.
No more than death regards the throb of time.
No more than love is caught in a net of rhyme.

Transplanting Ferns

For over twenty years we have been friends
and enemies and friends again. We four
have coupled and uncoupled, now, in more
configurations than the various fronds
on all these different types of ferns. My hands,
crumbling clods and sifting earth to pour
around the knotted roots, have met with your
hands, and in such diversity of bonds,
they cannot be uncoiled in memory,
but spread beneath our lives, a raveled skein
of joy and sorrow, each of us aware
of something growing that we cannot see.
Our talk is comfortable. "It looks like rain."
"That would be good." This is a kind of prayer.

The Back Way

You taught me this road, and I drive it this morning
to feel you with me, the rise and fall
of these mountains, the way they seem to breathe.

I drive without the radio,
attentive to details, not thinking. I watch
a turkey buzzard quivering over
a bowl of pine and redbud blush,
a cardinal quilting air in front of me.

Not thinking, I say. Not wondering
what I have lost.
I must make it enough: this sun, this slope
of blue phlox, this outcry
of forsythia.

Separate Vacation

You walk, some days, for hours. A boy pulls mud
sharks from the shallows, one by one, and leaves
them on the sand. They heave and flop a few
times, coat their bodies with a gritty bread-
ing, wait for death wide-eyed. One could believe
them capable of hate. Their eyes are blue.

Beneath the pier, the jellyfish propel
themselves behind their slimy spinnakers
in blindness, as though driven by remorse.
One bumps a piling with its purple bell,
nudges politely, finally defers,
and slides obliquely on its altered course.

Sandpipers run along the shore, distraught
with the responsibilities of birds.
Here is a souvenir: shard of a shell
inscribed like a tablet by water and salt
with marks that seem as meaningful as words.
The grief you cannot speak. The ebb and swell.

In a Bad Time

You have to get good and drunk
    to feel passion, and then
        there's that crumbling edge between
            sweetness and terrible sorrow

and sleep wanting you, too
    and probably in the morning
        you won't even remember
            how it was: an osprey dropping

stone-dense from deep sky
    to splinter the mirror of river
        (you could almost disbelieve it
            while it happened) and the fish

quivering in the claw, the bird
    shaking itself like a dog
        throwing a spangled shower
            as it struggled back to the sky

out of sight and over
    utterly irretrievable
        and beautiful nearly beyond
            enduring. Somehow, you do.

Veery

When you love, you open your soul
again and again: a strange, spilling music
you think you hear. But who could believe
it is always there? Every morning,

again and again, a strange, spilling music,
over coffee, in the garden, walking—
it is always there. Every morning,
every night. It is with you now,

over coffee, in the garden. Walking
in the forest, you are no longer afraid.
Every night it is with you. Now
you listen to hear the veery sing its ode

in the forest. You are no longer afraid.
"Listen," your grandmother says in a dream.
You listen. To hear the veery sing its ode
to grief! You welcome it inside. You

listen. Your grandmother says in a dream,
"When you love, you open your soul
to grief. You welcome it inside you."
You think you hear. But who could believe?

Watermark

All-but-invisible typography—
upper and lower case, ampersands
like curling vines—the way his hands
are letterpressed in the pulp of memory,
the way his voice coils in the fibered square
without so much as a whisper, not a word
or a lover's sigh, only the flat, furred
surface. *Tabula rasa.* Nothing there.
You use it for a list of Things to Do
Tomorrow, in that other life you lead,
the one in which you hardly ever need
to think of him. (You think he thinks of you
the same way: translucent, white on white.
He lifts you up. He holds you to the light.)

Birdhouse

Such a cunning cottage might
be called a home, could one compare
a bird to you or me. But there
you have it: one cannot quite.

Bird bones are hollow, a bird's heart
an oscillation in the air;
her dark eye is fixed somewhere
away. She may stay the night,

may even nest. May utter bright,
nearly domestic sounds. Where
this conceit leads is thin air.
Her business is flight.

Bob Thompson at the Piano

He offers you the melody, like bread
I watched my grandmother lift away from the oven—
a solid, shapely thing, so complete in itself
I could almost forget the way it came about:
the ceremony of the sprinkled yeast,
the necessary bit of something sweet,
the rhythm of the kneading and her voice,
a secret she told about her mother's mother,
who married someone, not the man she loved,
and how he came into the hardware store
when both of them were in their seventies
and took her in his arms at last, too late.

He offers you the melody, and then
he seems to simply let it rise, the way
Grandmother put the dough into a bowl,
covered it with a towel, untied her apron,
and told me to go outside, now, and play.
So I went swimming, or maybe I took the canoe
to that quiet cove on the far edge of the lake
where lily pads floated in a trembling layer,
my small heart full of my great-great-grandmother's ache,
crying a dead woman's tears, and wondering who
on earth I would have been, today,
had love prevailed, all those years ago.

He offers you the melody, like bread,
and pours the rest of the song around it, through
the spaces—honey and butter and cinnamon,
and you are a child again, you have nothing to do
except to lose yourself for a little while.
Start out in any direction. Wander. Stray
into the territory of dreams. Stay
as long as you please, and, when you please, return,
for the melody is always there, like bread,
like a woman in a kitchen, telling a story
with no clear lesson, from which a child could learn
the difference between eating and being fed.

Canoeing in Fog

We eased ourselves into the lake at nightfall,
paddled to the middle of the bowl,
and rested there, the water breathing under us.
I'd never been inside a cloud.
It was dark and bright at once.
Frog calls traced the shoreline.

Small bats whirled between us and veered away
like curious angels or promises we meant to keep.

Huckleberries

So Dorothy sent us off to Dolly Sods
with a plastic pint container and a lid
and promises of huckleberry muffins
in the morning. We found them where she'd said
we would, in a high and quiet place of spruce
and laurel, bushes as crowded with berries

as a country night with stars. So small. So blue.
Bluer than Prussian, bluer than indigo, bluer than
anything, color that looks right back at you
with the eyes of a long-forgotten, favorite doll.
Tiny as buttons on a doll's dress. So small,
and our fingers grown so clumsy, so fat, so adult.

Picture two middle-aged women, bent over, sweating,
plucking and talking, inhaling spruce and sky.
We grew up together, Julie. You remember
my birthday party the year we both were seven.
Your father used to keep track of us, you told me,
by listening to us, giggling, across the lake.

We didn't even pick a pint of berries,
and of course we stayed too long. The afternoon
went dim. We strayed into a boggy thicket
and lost our way, and blundered in the mud,
and then, like something out of a storybook
with a happy ending, found the path again.

Picture two middle-aged women, hugging and laughing,
telling each other we weren't really scared.
We ran straight down the mountain, ran all the way,
huckleberries bouncing in my backpack,
and leapt from rock to rock across Red Creek,
huckleberries jumping up and down for joy.

Burying Day

For Anita Skeen

The day before, I'd watched a nature film
about the earth's volcanic core—churning
molten mass below the crust you broke
with the cemetery shovel to plant
the pink geraniums your mother loved.
I thought, how small we are, how small
these compact bricks of ash and bone.

Still yet, as they say here, everything mattered:
the winding drive through West Virginia green
past blooming elderberries and catalpas,
country churches, yard sales sprawled on lawns;
our psalms and poems and wobbly harmonies;
the one-note bird in the cedar, like a bell;
dirt flung down into the hole;

the cemetery groundsman, large and gentle,
who took a picture of us beside the headstone.
Afterwards, the waitress at the restaurant
who called you Baby, the way a mother might;
and thunderstorms, two in one afternoon,
soaking the ground at Spring Hill and Kentuck,
cool water going deep, deep.

Sleeping in the Attic

It feels like a tent
or a Japanese temple,
tucked-in, well-met, rent-
free. No chairs or table.
A garret with a gable,

a lighthouse, a castle
tower, the cabin
of an ocean-sailing vessel,
the nest of a robin
adorned with a ribbon

or a cave in a cliff,
for rest after climbing,
where the Old Ones lived,
made love, lay dreaming.
Listen. A bell is chiming.

Calhoun County, September

Awakened by moonlight through leaded glass,
I, who sleep with my city windows draped,
in the third-story stratum between siren and jetscream:
astounded by quiet.

All day we cut glass, and my ears were filled
with the cutter's rasp, the cry of the breaking pane;
watery greens, and reds like wine or blood,
and smoky, throaty blues.

It is cold outside. Under the Milky Way
moon and dew are suspended in clear, brittle air;
across the valley, mist on a jagged line of ridge,
like skin on bone.

Far up the hollow, someone or something—
an animal in distress, or a night-flying bird—
calls out a single note.
I listen. Again.

The night takes it up, with harmonic and echo;
it rings down the hollow like water running a creekbed,
a cry like a crack as it travels through glass,
seeking but sure.

Past the Peak

Once again, the other side of fall.
Dusk. A cloud the color of wood smoke
clotted in a mesh of tarnished oak,
gibbous moon like a deflating ball
wobbling just above the mountain's brow.
Listen, there is something like relief
in this weather: trauma gone to grief,
slow and private, willing to allow
imperfection and perversity,
ragged leaves revolving to the stark
swing of a lopsided waltz. Today
autumn slips beyond its urgency
toward an umber grace. It will be dark
by the time I reach the place I stay.

At Winter Solstice

My lawn is deep in brittle maple leaves
huddled against the house, each curving spine
outlined with frost. My neighbor's holly tree,
old keeper of cardinals, old tower of green,
is standing watch, grandfatherly, in this
season of giving thanks and going home.
Come close: we need each other more, the less
directly we're regarded by the sun,
and the long night is on us now. Come
close as you can, my friend, and let us share
the stories we were saving for this time,
and take the measure of another year.
Come close, and let us watch the morning in:
the hour of turning to the light again.

Colleen Anderson is a writer, songwriter, and graphic designer who lives in Charleston, West Virginia. Her writing has appeared in *Redbook, Arts & Letters, Antietam Review*, and many other publications; two of her stories were nominated for the Pushcart Prize. Her songs have been featured on *Mountain Stage* and *The Folk Sampler*, and she has produced two collections of original songs. In 2012, her children's chapter book, *Missing: Mrs. Cornblossom*, won a Moonbeam Children's Book Award. Her writing has also earned two Individual Artist Fellowships from the WV Commission on the Arts and a residency fellowship from the Helene Wurlitzer Foundation of Taos, New Mexico.

About the cover art:

Del Webber, a second-generation rattan weaver, created the bound stone on the cover. His woven stones incorporate various knotting and weaving techniques and express his reverence for nature. In East Asian beliefs, stones can be imbued with special powers: the bound stone is symbolic of entry into another world.

CPSIA information can be obtained at www.ICGtesting.com
Printed in the USA
LVOW10s0302020716

494986LV00013BA/71/P